WOMEN OF
THE OLD WEST

JUDITH ALTER
WOMEN
OF THE OLD WEST

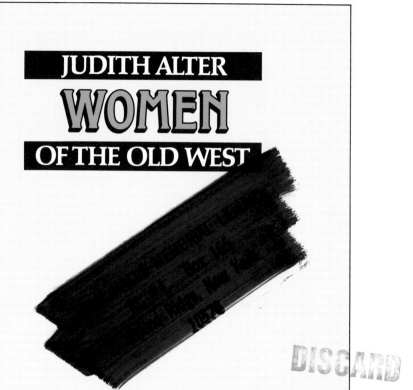

Franklin Watts
New York / London / Toronto / Sydney
A First Book / 1989

Cover photograph courtesy of the Granger Collection.

Photographs courtesy of: The Granger Collection: pp. 6, 9, 11 (top), 12, 16, 19, 26 (bottom), 46 (bottom), 51 (right), 54 (right); New York Public Library Picture Collection: pp. 8, 11 (bottom), 13, 23, 26 (top), 33, 35, 39 (bottom), 59; Amon Carter Museum, Fort Worth, Texas: pp. 20, 54 (left), 55; Custer Battlefield National Monument: p. 26 (top); Bettmann Archive: pp. 30, 51 (left); Culver Pictures: pp. 39 (top), 41; Wyoming State Archives, Museums and Historical Department: p. 46 (top); Western History Collections, University of Oklahoma Library: p. 18

Library of Congress Cataloging in Publication Data

Alter, Judy, 1938—
Women of the Old West / Judith Alter.
p. cm.—(A First book)
Bibliography: p.
Includes index.
Summary: Examines the various roles of women in the Old West, describing the living conditions and opportunities available to those women who broke the stereotypical picture of the tired settler's wife.
ISBN 0-531-10756-6
1. Women—West (U.S.)—History—Juvenile literature. 2. Pioneer women—West (U.S.)—History—Juvenile literature. 3. Frontier and pioneer life—West (U.S.)—Juvenile literature. [1. Women—West (U.S.)—History. 2. Frontier and pioneer life—West (U.S.) 3. West (U.S.)—History.] I. Title. II. Series.
HQ1438.W45A48   1989
305.4'2'09—dc19   88-34549   CIP   AC

CONTENTS

Life in the Old West was very difficult for pioneer families. They lived in isolated, dreary sod huts with the vast frontier surrounding them.

A MAN'S LAND

"The West was kind to men and dogs but hell on women and horses." So goes an old saying. The Old West, that land of adventure and freedom, was a man's land.

Photographs show weary-looking women, with children clutching their ragged skirts, standing in front of dismal sod huts—the expressions on their faces telling clearly what they think of life in the Old West. The settler's wife in the photograph is almost always a white woman. Overlooked are the native Americans who had always lived in the West and the Hispanic settlers who had come there centuries earlier. Also missing are black pioneers, many of whom homesteaded in Kansas and Oklahoma, and Chinese settlers who formed small communities around mining towns.

The first white men who went west were the mountain men who began to explore in the 1830s and 1840s, and they left their women behind them. So, too, the early settlers in most parts of the West were men without women.

But in the mid-1840s, the first wagon trains were rolling across the plains, leaving civilization behind at Independence, Missouri. The wagon trains carried families—women and children— seeking new homes in California and Oregon, the

In the mid-1840s, women and children began making the long, uncomfortable journey west in covered wagons.

Wagons were packed with most of
the household goods women would need
to set up their new homes.

two most common destinations for early pioneers. Most women only went west to follow their men-folk who were seeking a new home. For women, the trip was probably almost unbearable. They walked or rode in slow ox-drawn wagons that were crammed with household goods, leaving them almost no place to sit. Some walked behind ox-drawn carts, rather than wagons, and a large number of

Mormon women actually helped push handcarts from the Mississippi to Salt Lake City in the 1850s. Women carried children too young to walk, and worried constantly over those old enough to wander into mischief on the prairies.

Their clothes were inappropriate for the journey. Billowing full skirts blew around their heads and dragged in the mud; hoopskirts and bustles were equally impractical. Women learned to wear high-topped shoes to protect their feet, sunbonnets to keep off the burning rays, underdrawers for warmth in winter.

They found little privacy and no cosmetics. A good soaking bath was a rare luxury; more often, an outdoor stream was the tub, and western river water tended to be the color of dirty soapsuds. A broken piece of looking glass or a piece of tin was the only mirror. Women used sour milk or buttermilk as a skin bleach, white wax or spermaceti (whale) oil as a salve for their complexions, and a light dusting of cornstarch for face powder.

These early women were soon followed by a second wave of immigrants, women whose energies were not necessarily so taken up with survival. As the West was civilized, more and more women came, many alone, some in search of husbands, but others simply in search of new lives and new free-

There were
no comforts
or luxuries
available to
women crossing
the frontier in
covered wagons;
surviving the
journey was the
only goal.

As time passed and the frontier became
settled, more women traveled west alone on the
comfortable, efficient railroad system.

dom. Although most women chose traditional roles, working as laundresses, cooks, and teachers, many became shopkeepers, restauranteurs, lawyers, doctors, dentists, journalists, pawnbrokers, actresses, barbers, photographers, even mule skinners, and, yes, outlaws. By the 1870s, the West was a land of opportunity for women.

The opening of the West liberated many women. The newspaper editor at left proves she is capable of defending herself against a would-be attacker.

Another old saying about the West is that men tamed it and women civilized it. Women brought such small niceties as table manners, and the larger signs of civilization such as schools, churches, and other institutions. In the midst of rough mining towns and stark ranching communities, they formed women's clubs, set up libraries, planned lecture programs. Traveling theater shows of all kinds were common, and good literature was not rare.

The women, like their men, went west chasing the dream of a new life. Fortunately for us, they recorded their experiences in diaries, letters, articles, memoirs, and books. They left us a record of what it was like to be a woman in the Old West, that vast land stretching from the Mississippi River to California, from Texas to Montana.

THE MADONNA OF THE PRAIRIES

Artists and historians have called her "the Madonna of the Prairies," that homesteader's wife who fought desperately to keep a dirty sod house clean, swept a dirt floor to rid it of loose dirt, hung cheesecloth to keep dirt and bugs from dropping from a dirt roof into the food. She cooked huge meals, plowed alongside her husband, had her babies in the afternoon so she could put supper on the table at night, and feared more than anything a capture by Indians.

"Indians have burned your house. Come immediately." In 1884 when Nannie Alderson received that message, she had just given birth to her first daughter in Miles City, Montana, a hundred miles from her ranch. Nannie was from a wealthy West Virginia family and was used to luxuries and servants. Visiting an aunt in Kansas, she met Walter

The homesteader's wife tried desperately to provide everything her family would need.

Alderson, a minister's son who had run away at the age of thirteen to be a cowboy.

After their wedding, Walter took his bride back to Montana. Her first home was a dirt-roofed cabin. There was one window and a dirt floor covered by a clean wagon canvas.

There were no other women close enough to visit, though Indians often came to beg food. Nannie dealt with rattlesnakes, hard water for wash, clothes that were never again white. She raised a garden and dressed freshly butchered meat, and after one year, she had a new, four-room house with built-in cupboards, new walnut furniture, and flowered wallpaper.

Nannie Alderson followed her man west out of love, but some historians suggest that marriage in the nineteenth century was often less for love than for building a family or farm. Certainly, some women were mail-order brides, journeying to marry, sight unseen, men who advertised for them and paid their way west. Still other women homesteaded on their own land; in some parts of the West, an unbelievably large number of lone women homesteaded property in their own name.

There were also a surprising number of black women, but they remained largely invisible on the frontier. Many went west as slaves, and their treatment, even after emancipation, varied from state to state.

Biddy Mason was typical of former slaves who found prosperity out West. She traveled by wagon train from Mississippi to California in 1851, driving her master's sheep behind his wagon. But when he decided to leave California in 1854, Biddy convinced the sheriff to issue a writ preventing him from taking his slaves, including herself and her three

A black immigrant family on the prairie.

daughters, out of the state. In 1856, Biddy won her freedom through the courts, and in the 1860s, she began buying real estate. Eventually, her $250 investment multiplied many times over, and she spent her later years helping other immigrant black families.

Black or white, married or single, the frontier woman's biggest fear was capture by Indians. Some captives who were returned to civilization either by rescue or ransom later wrote about their experiences or even went on the lecture circuit. They became highly popular, catching the public fancy in a horrifying way. Those few who made public their experience gathered so much attention that people back East believed women were captured by the hundreds. Actually, although many women were killed in conflicts with Indians, not as many were taken captive as is generally believed.

Indians were sometimes provoked into attacking wagon trains trespassing on their territory.

The painting above, done by Carl Wimer in 1855, illustrates the abduction of a frontier woman by Indians.

Perhaps the best-known memoir of an Indian captive is Fanny Kelly's *Narrative of My Captivity among the Sioux Indians.* Fanny Kelly was nineteen years old and married nine months, when she set out with a handful of immigrants from Wyoming's Fort Laramie in July 1864. The army had declared the way safe, but the small train had gone less than 80 miles when they were attacked by 250 Ogallala Sioux. Although her husband escaped, most men of the party were killed. Fanny and her five-year-old stepdaughter, Mary, were captured along with the other women and children. The child was later killed after trying to escape.

Most white women swore they would prefer death to captivity, but not Fanny. She held on to the hope of rescue throughout her captivity. Every time the Indians tried to tattoo her, she fainted. They might have killed her as a coward had she not, in an extraordinary act of bravery, saved another white woman who was about to be killed because she wailed all the time. Ottawa, a chief, was impressed, and Fanny became his property.

The Sioux were really fond of Fanny and reluctant to release her, in spite of pressure from the army. Fanny Kelly became a political prize. When she was acquired by Blackfeet Sioux, Fanny suspected they wanted to use her to attack Fort Sully. She smuggled a letter to the army by means of yet another young, lovestruck Indian. Finally, accompanied by 1,000 mounted warriors, she was peacefully returned to the white settlement.

The West was full of other dangers for the Madonna of the Prairies—she endured drought, prairie fire, fierce storms, and illness with no care available. Although Indian captivity seems the most dramatic story to come out of her experience, the truth about the homesteader's life may have more real drama.

LAUNDRESSES AND LADIES

Homesteaders' wives weren't the only ones to follow men west. When the army moved onto the plains after the Civil War—their mission was to deal with Indian uprisings once and for all—they brought with them a separate army of women. Two distinct groups stand out in history

The first was the laundresses. The only women officially recognized as part of a garrison, they took in washing as a business. The row of houses where they lived became known as Soapsuds Row. The laundresses received housing, food, fuel, payment, and other benefits from the army. Many of the women were married to enlisted men, and their pay far exceeded that of their husbands. Most of them were uneducated, but good, honest, hardworking women.

The other group—officers' wives—were at the other end of the social scale, their lives totally different from those of the laundresses, but also

Laundresses, hard-working women who took in
washing as a business, made large sums of money.

difficult. They were moved from post to post frequently, perhaps going from the comforts of the East to the searing desolation of Fort Yuma in Arizona and then to the bitter cold of a Montana winter.

Housing for officers generally ranged from barely acceptable to awful, and many officers' wives lived in places that would have made the settlers' sod huts look like palaces. Quarters were often insect-infested cottonwood log cabins with dirt floors, or drafty board houses through which the winter wind whistled unobstructed.

Life was often difficult for these women, especially when they waited for the return of husbands out on patrol. But there were compensations, including a fairly active social life. Activities at any army post might include games, band concerts, card parties, amateur theatricals, sewing bees, skating, sleighing in winter, lawn tennis in milder seasons, croquet, hunting for prairie chickens and grouse, long rides on the prairie.

Army wives were always thought to be in great danger from Indians, although, after 1861, there is not one instance recorded of a woman killed at an army post by Indians. They actually were in more danger from their overprotective husbands. General George Armstrong Custer made it plain to his officers that the one in charge of his wife was to shoot her in case of attack. Once Elizabeth (Libbie) Custer was with a detachment of 50 men that was attacked by 600 Indians. After a three-hour battle, the Indians withdrew, but the colonel in charge told Elizabeth he had been preparing to shoot her. "Would you have given me no chance for life in case the battle had gone in your favor?" she asked. "Not one," he said.

Mrs. Custer left probably the best record of life as an army officer's wife during that period in her book, *Tenting on the Plains*. In a thick, factual journal, she recorded beauty where most would have seen none, writing that a "rarely exultant feeling takes possession of one in the gallops over the Plains" and guessing that "the sky fits close down all around" surely was said of the plains. Still, she also wrote of dreary trips over monotonous country only to end in a small post of log huts. And she described Kansas as "hot, blistered earth, dry beds of streams, and soil apparently so barren that not even the wild flowers would bloom . . . add pestilence, Indians and an undisciplined mutinous soldiery. . . ."

Like most army wives, life for Libbie was full of terrors, both real and imaginary. New to the Plains, she experienced a prairie storm, describing herself

*Above: Army officers'
wives usually had
active social lives.
In this photo, General
George Armstrong Custer
and his wife, Elizabeth,
are shown gathered
in their home with
some friends.*

*Left: Elizabeth Bacon
Custer in a photograph
taken in 1855.*

as "quaking and terrified under the covers . . . alone in a tent, a kind of 'rag house' which might have been a handkerchief."

There were, of course, Indians to worry about too. Once Libbie and another woman walked out of their quarters at dusk. They were mistaken for Indians in the near darkness and nearly shot at by sentries. The enlisted man with them ordered the two women to lie in the grass to avoid being fired upon while he crept back to the post. For Libbie, the terror of being left alone in the darkness was almost worse than being fired at.

The worst ordeal, however, was the anxiety of the expeditions. Any vision of the dashing trooper in a gay uniform faded before the reality of men marching out on an Indian campaign. Following her husband's departure, there were "days of anxiety, and nights of hideous dreams of what might befall him." When he once returned unexpectedly, she wrote "There was in that summer of 1867 one long, perfect day. It was mine, and—blessed be our memory . . . it is still mine, for time and for eternity."

For Libbie Custer, her days on the frontier ended as they did for far too many army wives—with the death of her husband. The Battle of the Little Bighorn, known among the Plains Indians as the Battle of Greasy Grass, was the last major victory for the Indians. Although it has gone down in white history as a massacre, it demonstrated the Indians' determination to defend their land and way of life. For a long time, Custer was considered the martyr-hero of the battle, but recent study has changed his reputation, and he is now considered to have foolishly led his men into a position they could not defend.

But Libbie was made of stern stuff. When word was brought to her of Custer's death, she threw a wrap over her dressing gown and accompanied the captain to the twenty-five other widows of that battle to offer them consolation.

TEACHER, DOCTOR, LAWYER

The schoolmarm is almost as much a standard figure in our picture of the Old West as the homesteader's wife. We see her before a rough log schoolhouse, her pupils clustered around her. In the movies, we see her fall in love with the rugged cowboy. She is always an Easterner, usually quite dainty, and often a little overwhelmed by the wild life of the West.

The schoolteacher is not an invention of western novels and movies. There were hundreds and hundreds of them, and they were probably the first women to go west alone, independent of a man. Their importance in civilizing the West is beyond question.

Female teachers went west in amazing numbers. Some went because they were dedicated to teaching and saw the great need in the West; many went because they were hoping to meet a husband.

They taught for miserable pay—sometimes only $12.00 per month and board, sometimes $1.00 per student per month and board. The board provided usually meant that the teacher stayed one week with one family, the next with another, and so on, until she had been passed around the community and was ready to begin the circle again. Since the families of most pupils lived in tiny one-room cabins, already crowded, boarding around was a horror. Teachers were often homesick and lonely. They were often forbidden to marry, and the social activities they were allowed were meager.

They were also sometimes as young as fifteen, not much older than their pupils. They seldom had textbooks, but taught instead from hymnals, almanacs, and whatever books their pupils' families could provide. Classroom seats might be no more than two boards balanced on rocks, and the blackboard simply a painted piece of wood. In the early years, no one teacher had many pupils, but as the

The prairie "schoolmarm" was often a young and dainty Easterner who traveled west alone.

settlement of the West increased, it was not unusual for one teacher to be responsible for fifty to
sixty students.

Teachers may have been the first and most nu-
merous of the independent women to go west, but
they were soon followed by other professionals—
doctors and lawyers. In the late 1800s, women physicians were frowned upon in the West just as they
were in other parts of the country. The work was
considered too nasty and intimate for women; at
the very least, it was thought they should confine
themselves to treating other women. Still, women
were generally the ones who gave medical aid when
it was needed. The Indian and Mexican-American
cultures thought women were gifted with special
healing powers. Among Anglo women, midwifery
and nursing were fairly common occupations,
though usually unpaid.

But by the 1870s, there were a fair number of
women physicians scattered throughout the West,
many with regular medical licenses. Frequently,
they were also called upon to serve as everything
from dentist to undertaker.

Typical of such women was Georgia Arbuckle
Fix, the lone woman in the 1883 graduating class at
the State University of Omaha's College of Medi-

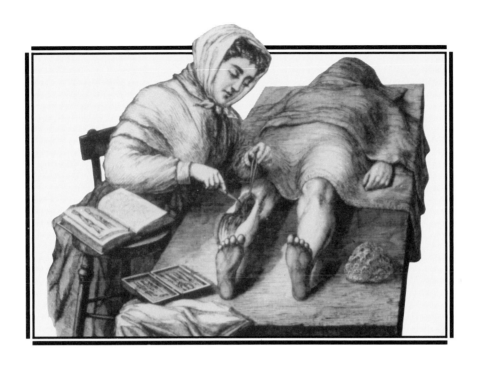

*By the late nineteenth century, there were
a fair number of women physicians in the west. Above:
a woman studies the anatomy of the human leg.*

cine in Nebraska. Dr. Fix practiced on the North Platte River in western Nebraska.

Dr. Fix soon became a familiar figure, riding out on calls. It was not unusual for cowboys to break an arm or a leg, and she set their bones, depending on other cowboys to hold the patient still and on the patient to bear the pain quietly. Dr. Fix followed the roads of the day—sometimes cattle trails, sometimes simply the easiest way across the prairie. Like many pioneer women, she seemed to possess an uncanny sense of direction. She could start out across the prairie and go directly to the claim or farm where she was needed. In good weather, she rode in a buggy; in a storm, she simply unhitched the horse and rode it.

There were no dentists and few preachers in the Nebraska territory, and Dr. Fix was called upon to fill both roles, frequently yanking a tooth out of a cowboy who could no longer stand the pain. It was a more serious thing to be called upon to be preacher, but when she lost a patient and there was no one else available, Dr. Fix said the last prayer over the grave.

Doctors in those days had no set fees. A ledger used by Dr. Fix shows figures varying from fifty cents to four dollars for either medicine or treatment. She probably charged only what she thought the patient could pay and was often paid with chickens, eggs, butter, fresh-picked wild fruit, even cattle.

There were even fewer women lawyers than doctors in the Old West. In California in 1878, law restricted the legal profession to "any male white citizen," but Clara Shortridge Foltz challenged it. Before studying law, Foltz had lectured on women's

*A few determined women challenged local laws
and ventured into the legal profession.*

equality and suffrage and, in 1876, had divorced her husband, the father of her five children. She was not exactly a reticent, shy female when she sought an apprenticeship in a law firm. At first, she was given the usual statement: "A woman's place is in the home, unless it is as a teacher." Eventually, however, she read law—law school was not necessary in those days. Before she could practice, though, the state law would have to be changed, so Foltz wrote a new statute and persuaded a legislator to sponsor it. Men claimed women would hear indelicate testimony in court, inappropriate for their dainty ears. The bill barely passed the legislature and Foltz had to sneak into the governor's office to persuade him to sign it, but she was licensed to practice law in 1878. She specialized in divorce and inheritance cases, but felt the need to attend a formal school of law. Once again, Clara Foltz had to fight a battle, this time for admission to Hastings College of Law in San Francisco. This battle went all the way to the state's supreme court before Clara won. Eventually, she developed a highly successful practice in criminal law and was active in reforming the California criminal justice system.

WOMEN ON THE STAGE

Women remained scarce in the West for much of the nineteenth century, and their social company was much valued by the men. In some mining camps, there were so few women that they were rationed among the men—even at socials, no one man was allowed to monopolize a woman for long. Women loved the community affairs—the more energy required, the better. There were musicales, box suppers, weddings, barn raisings, and ranch parties. It was nothing for a woman, properly accompanied by one or more men, to ride horseback or in a buggy for forty miles to a dance. In northern climates, if it snowed all night, the people danced all night and went home in the morning if the snowdrifts permitted. National holidays were regularly celebrated, and even religious events—camp meetings and outdoor revivals—were as social in nature as they were devotional. Nobody enjoyed a good time more than a western woman.

But no matter how inclined they were to fun, there just weren't enough women in the West. One result of this was that actresses became very popular.

A woman on a stage could, in a sense, be shared by a whole audience of men. There were five times as many actresses for the population in the West as in the East at the same time, and many single women gained fame on the stages of the frontier. The demand for female performers was so great that young women even played male roles.

Frontier men went to the theater just to see the women. And though they were enthusiastic, western men were not always uncritical. Rowdy male audiences out west demanded entertainment—they wanted a rollicking good time, and they loved the spectacular. They did not tolerate poor performances. Sometimes they took the offending actress, tossed her in a blanket, and ushered her out of town.

Lola Montez was probably the most talked about stage performer of the West in her time. In spite of her Spanish-sounding name, Lola was born in Ireland. She was a teenage runaway who had an early and unfortunate marriage followed by a colorful career as a Spanish dancer. Her career in London

*Miners
enjoying a
variety show at
Cripple Creek,
Colorado*

Lola Montez

ended in 1843 after her Scottish/Irish ancestry was revealed, and she left the stage amid hisses and boos. In the early 1850s she came to America and decided to try her luck out west. Her debut in San Francisco was so popular that tickets sold for $65.00 each, an enormous amount of money in those days.

Lola left a legacy of sorts in the form of a young actress named Lotta Crabtree. Lotta was a young child in Grass Valley (California) when Lola Montez retired to that community. Lola taught the child to ride, dance, and sing. With red hair in long curls, flashing black eyes, and a voice full of laughter, Lotta first went on the public stage at the age of eight, doing an Irish jig. The miners loved her.

By the time she was in her teens, in the 1860s, Lotta was baring her legs and smoking on stage. It was unladylike, but Lotta got away with it because her admirers were convinced it was all in a spirit of childish innocence. Lotta emphasized this image by finishing each performance clad in white, singing a tear-jerking ballad. Miners and proper ladies both adored her.

Serious drama was less popular in the West than the eye-catching spectacles offered by Lola, Lotta, and others like them. In 1881, the famed French actress Sarah Bernhardt appeared in *Camille* in St. Joseph, Missouri, and one critic complained

Left: Miss Lotta Crabtree followed in the footsteps of Lola Montez and entertained proper ladies and miners alike.

that she was "distressingly ugly . . . with arms as long and wiry as the tendrils of devil fish."

But as the West grew more settled and civilized, its citizens' taste in theater grew more formal. By 1890, neither Lola nor Lotta would have been tolerated by theater patrons who looked forward to an evening in the theater as a proper social occasion and expected to be rewarded with a serious offering. The rough miners who cheered and stamped their approval were replaced by well-dressed men and women who clapped politely.

BATTLEAXES AND REFORMERS

Without the women to give a sense of community, law in many parts of the West might have remained an every-man-for-himself kind of vigilante justice even longer than it did. But the women brought that necessary sense of community and family.

Once the first generation of women had mastered survival on the prairie, their followers also looked beyond survival. Women were in the forefront of many reform movements in the American West, giving their all to a variety of causes. Once the frontier had been tamed, women were determined to shape its future and they took up causes. Men criticized them for stepping outside the home, but the women were not daunted.

Two women provide excellent examples of reformers on the frontier. One, Esther Hobart McQuigg Morris, is a heroine of women's suffrage.

The other, Carry Nation, has become a cartoon figure in the national imagination, going throughout the land swinging her axe against alcohol. Few realize that most of Carry Nation's battles were fought in the West.

Women in the West earned the right to vote before their eastern sisters. The territory of Wyoming in 1869 became the first government in the world to grant women the right to vote. When Wyoming was admitted to the union in 1890, there were still no states with political rights for women; Wyoming refused to come in without the women. Some claim that the women's vote in Wyoming was won by Esther Hobart McQuigg Morris.

Esther Morris was fifty-five years old, six feet tall, widowed and remarried—an independent woman—when she hosted a famous tea party in South Pass City, then the largest city in Wyoming. The story goes that Morris invited two legislative candidates to tea, seeking their pledge that they would support suffrage. Both men pledged their support. After his 1869 election, William Bright, the winner, introduced a suffrage bill in the Wyoming legislature. The founding fathers of the state, thinking the bill would encourage settlement and publicize Wyoming, passed the bill. Not only did the law allow women the vote, it provided that they could own property, earn and keep money, serve on juries, and retain guardianship of minor children, all rights previously denied them.

In 1870, Esther Morris became the country's first female justice of the peace. The previous officeholder had retired, saying sarcastically that women could hold the office now that they had the vote. Esther Morris held court in a log cabin and ordered guns left outside the door. When her saloon-keeper husband, John, objected to her new role and made a scene, she fined him; when he refused to pay, she sent him to jail. In eight and a half months in office, Esther Morris ruled on seventy decisions (some records say only forty), and none were later overruled. Esther Morris saw her position as a test of women's ability, and she passed that test with flying colors.

The western states led the nation in giving the vote to women, and by the time women's suffrage was added to the Constitution in 1920, women throughout the West were already voting, except in Texas and New Mexico.

Carry Nation is a more familiar figure than Esther Morris, even though the reform for which she fought has been less enduring. Carry Nation was tall, nearly six feet, and she dressed all in black,

The formidable Esther Morris, a champion of women's suffrage

Carry Nation crusaded to outlaw liquor in the West. In this cartoon, she holds her trademark axe, which gained her much public attention.

with a black bonnet on her head. Her hatchet or axe earned her public attention and became her trademark as she fought for temperance, the outlawing of all liquor.

Her first attack upon a barroom came in 1900 in the Hotel Carey in Wichita, Kansas. Only a scattering of men were drinking in the bar when Carry marched in armed with a cane, an iron rod, and some large stones. She smashed all the bottles and a $1,500 mirror, caned the drinkers, and got herself arrested.

She closed all the saloons in Medicine Lodge, Kansas, and moved on through the rest of the state. Liquor was so common in Kansas that the term ''bootlegger'' is said to have originated there because men carried bottles in their boots. Carry smashed those hidden bottles too and was even known to jerk cigars and cigarettes from men's mouths in public.

Carry Nation spent the rest of her life smashing saloons, touring and lecturing for her cause, and knocking cigars out of men's mouths. The end of her career came in Butte, Montana, when she invaded a saloon owned by a woman, one May Loy, who, hatchet in hand, chased Nation out into the street as she approached. Carry Nation never smashed another bottle.

THE OUTLAW TRAIL

Inevitably, there were women in the West who rode the outlaw trail. Some folks have suggested that the rough surroundings of the Old West—without law, order, and refined society—turned these women into outlaws.

A long list of them could be compiled—Cattle Kate, Rose of the Cimarron, Cattle Annie, Little Britches, Pearl Hart—but two of the most notorious were Belle Starr and Calamity Jane. Belle Starr spent one stretch in jail and was generally considered to be a horse and cattle thief. Calamity Jane was less likely an outlaw than simply an outrageous eccentric, but because of her rough and rowdy nature, she is generally classed with the female "bad guys" of the West.

Belle Starr was born Myra Belle Shirley in northwestern Arkansas. Beyond that one fact about her life, it is difficult to separate folklore from fact. Legend has it that she was from a family of aristocratic Virginians who had settled in Missouri and who rode with the infamous Southern guerrilla Quantrill on his raids with a gang that supposedly included the outlawed James brothers. One of her brothers rode with Quantrill and legend says Belle once strapped on a pistol too. In truth, she probably did no more than a little spying. When her brother was killed by Yankees during the Civil War, the family moved to Texas. There Belle met up with former Quantrill raiders—only now they were outlaws, robbing banks and railroad trains.

In every story about her, Belle's name is linked with the famed outlaw Cole Younger, but the link is uncertain and Younger denied it. Still, he is often suggested as the father of her daughter, Pearl. Belle was, however, married to Jim Reed, who also had outlaw ways and was killed in 1874.

Belle next married Sam Starr, who was three-quarters Cherokee and who also had outlaw ways. They lived in Oklahoma where their home was a haven for outlaws. To Sam goes credit for Belle's only arrest—with him, she was accused of stealing horses and sentenced, by Judge Isaac Parker, the famed "Hanging Judge," to two six-month terms. Her only conviction also brought the biggest publicity of her life. Once freed, she returned to Oklahoma with Starr, but he was killed in a shootout at a dance.

Belle's life continued to be filled with outlaws. Her last husband, Jim July, had an old horse-stealing charge against him. Belle was never again arrested, although the general assumption is that she was involved in enough robbings and killings to fill a book. She did, however, meet an untimely end, ambushed while riding along an Oklahoma road. The killer was never found, though suspicion was focused on a neighbor Belle had threatened.

Calamity Jane is probably the boldest example of western women who declared their independence from men. She was supposedly born in Missouri of a good family. The story of how she went west is blurred, but Calamity is most associated with Deadwood, South Dakota, and with Wild Bill Hickok whom she claimed as her husband. Hickok denied the attachment, but Calamity is buried next to him in Deadwood.

A big woman, tall and muscular, Calamity was known to enjoy the company of men more than women, and she could ride and shoot like a man. In Deadwood, she took in washing, cared for sick families, probably was a bartender, worked with railroad crews, and often dressed like a man. She was also an alcoholic, which may explain the fan-

Belle Starr

Calamity Jane

tasy life she created for herself. She claimed to have been a teamster on a scientific expedition and boasted of having scouted for Custer. Wagon freighter was another occupation she claimed, and certainly she cussed like those legendary men who drove teams of horses or mules pulling freight across the western landscape and who could turn the air blue with their language.

But Calamity apparently turned people away from her with her outrageous behavior and outright lies. She died alone, lonely and bitter, and her life was not anything like the sentimental version portrayed in movies or in fiction.

Belle probably stole horses and cattle but was only convicted once in her life; Calamity was never convicted of a crime, indeed not really suspected. Yet both are known as outlaws, perhaps proving that women, like men, are known by the company they keep.

RANCH WOMEN AND COWGIRLS

In the Old West it could not be assumed that a woman was an outlaw just because she could do a man's work from the saddle or shoot straight and true. Many ranch wives worked as hard as their menfolk, often because the work was there to do and there was no one else to do it. Sometimes, though, they did it for the love of the freedom. If ranch wives were not outlaws, neither were they cowgirls. A true ranch woman would have been insulted to be called a cowgirl.

Cowgirls, those stars of Wild West Shows, did not really appear on the scene until almost 1900. Some learned to ride and rope on the family ranch; others had never been near a ranch or even a horse until they joined the show. In some ways, though, the cowgirl grew out of the ranch woman, for she made public what ranch women had proved out of

Cowgirls proved women could handle men's work and retain their femininity.

Below: Annie Oakley, a famous cowgirl, featured on a Buffalo Bill Wild West Show poster.

daily necessity: that women could do a man's work and still be women.

The real ranch women are, of course, less well known. One of the best-loved ranch women in all the West was Molly Goodnight, a Texas woman known as the Mother of the Panhandle. Molly mar-

Because of the quantity of work, ranch women had to work as hard as their male counterparts.

ried Goodnight in 1870 and in 1877 they settled in the Palo Duro Canyon in Texas. Molly drove the wagon while the men herded the cattle on the long trip from Colorado to the High Plains of Texas. Her new home was in a canyon 1,500 feet deep, 10 miles wide, and 100 miles long. Her nearest neighbor was 200 miles away.

But Molly was busy. She doctored the cowboys when needed, cooked for the entire ranch, gave spiritual comfort when that was needed, and welcomed wandering cowboys, hungry hunters, and starving Indians. The cowboys told the Indians that the "god who sent messages" (the post office) was in her home and, afraid, they never bothered her.

A ranch woman who made a name for herself with the skills of men was Lucille Mulhall. Lucille's family had a ranch in Oklahoma, and Lucille learned to ride, rope, and shoot as well as any man by doing real ranch work. She went on, though, to become the star of her father's Wild West Show.

Her father, Colonel Zack Mulhall, organized a show to entertain at various carnivals and fairs. Lucille gathered most of the attention in the show, including the eye of vice-presidential candidate Theodore Roosevelt who visited the Mulhall ranch and asked Lucille if she could rope a wolf. Three hours later, she reappeared dragging a dead wolf behind her horse. That was probably when Teddy Roosevelt coined the term "cowgirl."

Lucille gained a lot of attention, once roping eight horses simultaneously. She rode in the 1901 inaugural parade for President McKinley and Vice President Roosevelt, participated in steer roping contests where she beat all the men against whom she was competing, and once chased her steer over a five-foot fence in a roping contest. She was tiny and pretty, which made her rodeo accomplishments all the more amazing.

A LAND FOR WOMEN TOO

Life for women in the Old West was much more than an exhausting trip across the prairie and a dreary daily existence in a sod hut.

Teacher, actress, doctor, cowgirl, free spirit—the thread that runs through all their lives is freedom, the freedom to make choices about their lives, their careers, their marriages. Many women chose careers in fields usually open only to men. Others chose to end unsatisfactory marriages through divorce. Perhaps we think of divorce and careers as unusual in that day and age because we think of eastern models; women who lived in New York or Ohio or Virginia simply didn't have the same freedom to make choices. They were bound by society, by conventions that didn't affect their sisters in the West.

Women who took advantage of the freedom of the West were also distinguished by a sense of

Western women had the opportunity and freedom
to make many choices in their lives because they
had less pressure from society. Through their
hard work, determination, and positive spirits,
they are credited with civilizing the West.

hope. They looked to the bright future that the land of opportunity offered them. Men often wrote despairingly to families back east of the difficulties and dangers of the West; women were determined to endure and, in the end, to win. Most of them adapted to the harsh conditions and endless prairie and expected things to get better. One petticoat pioneer wrote, "Do not think I regret coming. No, far from it. I would not go back for the world. I am contented and happy, notwithstanding I sometimes get very hungry and weary."

FOR FURTHER READING

Alderson, Nannie T. and Helena Huntington Smith. *A Bride Goes West.* Lincoln, NE: University of Nebraska Press, 1969.

Brown, Dee. *The Gentle Tamers,* New York: Bantam Books, 1974.

Darling, Amanda. *Lola Montez.* New York: Stein and Day, 1972.

Jordan, Teresa. *Cowgirls: Women of the American West, An Oral History.* New York: Doubleday, 1984.

Ray, Grace Ernestine, *Wily Women of the West.* San Antonio, TX: The Naylor Company, 1972.

Roach, Joyce Gibson. *The Cowgirls.* Houston, TX: Cordovan Corporation, 1977.

Shirley, Glenn. *Belle Starr and Her Times.* Norman, OK: University of Oklahoma Press, 1982.

Time-Life Books, eds. with text by Joan Swallow Reiter. *The Women,* in series entitled *The Old West.* Alexandria, VA: Time-Life Books, 1978.

Western Writers of America, eds. *Women Who Made the Old West.* New York: Doubleday, 1980; Avon Books, 1981.

INDEX